The New Poly-Olbion

The New Poly-Olbion

Topographical Excursions

by

Andrew Young

*With an Introductory Account of the
Poet's Early Days*

Rupert Hart-Davis Limited
Upper James Street
1967

Printed in Great Britain at
The Bowering Press, Plymouth

Rupert Hart-Davis Limited
1–3 Upper James Street London W1

Contents

EARLY DAYS

EARLY DAYS

Doctor Johnson had a poor opinion of Elgin, but I was charmed when I paid it a visit. And the surrounding country has been praised by those best qualified to appreciate natural scenery, at least better qualified than I am. By the Water Poet, 'the most pleasant, and plentifull countrey in all Scotland'; by Lugless Willie Lithgow, 'the delectable planure of Murry, a second Lombardy'; by John Macky, 'the Vale of Evesham is not comparable to it'. I could not have chosen a better place to be born, in Scotland at least, unless it had been Kirkcudbright.

But my memories begin at Edinburgh. I remember a night full of lights and sounds and a throng of people; I was taken to an Exhibition, no doubt to see the illuminations. But my first clear recollection is of standing at the street door of our flat, proud of my new coat; I deserved the Scottish form of my name, Dandy. A man approached and said, 'Is your mother at home, sonny?' and when I nodded, 'Then run upstairs and tell her that a gentleman wants to speak to her. But wait; I'll hold your coat till you come back.' When I appeared before my mother, she had a great desire to speak to the gentleman.

Though my parents were not poor, they were careful; unlike most children I did not receive the Saturday penny. But I was not deprived of sweets; before going to bed at night I was given a piece of chocolate for swallowing a spoonful of cod-liver oil, and during the sermon in church sweets, called pan-drops, were passed along the pew. I do not remember being given toys; I had to make my own toys out of a newspaper, 'the men' as they were called. They were all profile, no arms and one leg, but their shapes were in some way suggestive. A thin man was likely to be a fast runner, but how fast depended on some subtlety in the shape. When my brother, older than I, experimenting with one, tore off a tiny fragment, I was furious and fell on him with my fists; he had maimed for life one of my best football forwards. Playing football on the floor was 'the men's' favourite occupation; it was the only place in Scotland where football was played on a Sunday evening, my mother allowing it, while my father attended church. Yet I must have received some toys, for after his death I found in his desk a little wooden engine which I seemed to remember. He had kept it there for more than fifty years.

> How gladly would the man recall to life
> The boy's neglected sire! a mother too,
> That softer friend, perhaps more gladly still,
> Might he demand them at the gates of death.

'The men' survived in a strange way, not as pieces of paper, but as names. These, too, could be suggestive. In a cricket team a name like Clackmannan, long and quickly said, might suggest a fast bowler with a long run, while a name like Galloway with three slow syllables might suggest a slow tricky bowler. Of course, 'the men' were not named after places in Scotland; they had their own names. And it was not in Scotland they lived, but on an island in the Atlantic, called in fact the Island. It had six universities, which apparently served no other purpose than to produce cricket and football teams. Tennis was despised in Edinburgh in those days, and it would not have been exciting to watch a game of golf. Games could be played in daylight, perhaps when I was on a cycling tour, but usually I watched them from my bed at night. Occasionally a selected team went on tour, but I could not follow their games well, unfamiliar with their foreign opponents. The Island became noted throughout the world for sport; and no wonder; all the best cricket and football teams visited the Island and all were beaten. Anthony Trollope had no need of 'men'; 'I myself was always my own hero; I was a very clever person, and beautiful young women used to be fond of me.' I played an even prouder part, god of the Island; at times it seemed almost blasphemous.

My education was late in beginning; while John Stuart Mill was taught Greek by his father at the age of three, my father did not teach me Latin till I was four. A year later I went to school, having to learn other things than Latin, such as the history and geography of Scotland, with England coming into the picture. Perhaps conditions in the school were primitive. We wrote on a slate with a slate pencil; some boys cleaned their slate with a sponge, others spat and rubbed. When not reading or writing we sat bolt-upright with arms crossed, motionless except to hold up a hand in response to a question. As we answered rightly or wrongly, we might go up or down the class. The boy who ended the day at the top was dux and went home with a silver medal round his neck, which he brought back next morning. I was seldom so decorated.

My father had a small library, not so much a good collection of books as a collection of good books, such as Baxter's *Saints' Rest* and Law's *Serious Call*; but it was not strong in poetry. Perhaps his feeling for it had been chilled by his familiarity with the Metrical Psalms, though something can be said for lines like

> Pure to the pure, froward thou kythst
> Unto the froward wight.

My own interest in poetry was confined to children's hymns, my favourite being Andrew Young's *There is a happy land*. That showed good taste, for the first stanza is given in the Oxford Book of Quotations. But suddenly my interest took a forward bound; I discovered among my father's books the Works of Shakespeare. It was an expurgated edition called The Household. Looking into it, I discovered that the famous English poet could not even rhyme his lines. Thinking I could do better I began a play in verse, *Hector or The Highland Chieftain*. Perhaps the subject did not lend itself to dramatic treatment, for I did not make much progress. I was more successful with a poem, *The Battle of Bannockburn*, for I remember the closing lines:

They fell, they fell,
Till there were few to tell
How the great battle was ended.

If these lines were the first to be written, they were the last to be published. They appear in an anthology, *The Wind and the Rain*, a footnote saying 'Aged 5'. If poets are born, not made, my attempt to write poetry may have begun too late.

About the age of eight I went to another school, where I again began to learn Latin. Along with *mensa mensae mensae mensam* two things in particular remain in my mind, two things I was told, one true, the other untrue. On a visit to our class Mr. Andrews, the headmaster, asked us questions. When I rose and answered one, he laid his hand on my head and, looking me in the face, said, 'My boy, you will grow up to stand one day in the pulpit.' What was untrue was what Mr Wallace, our teacher, told us about the word 'news'; he said it was made up of the first letters of North, East, West and South. I believed it at the time and it started my interest in words. My mother bought for me at an auction sale a dictionary in four large volumes, the Imperial. A faded photograph shows me as a child with curls riding a hobby-horse; I have been riding hobby-horses all my life and, while I have kept on changing horses, a favourite hobby has been with words. Why is a butterfly called a butterfly? What is the connexion between infant and infantry? It pleased me to know things that others might not know, as, for example, that there is no connexion between island and isle, sorrow and sorry, trifle and trivial. One can always learn something new about words. At the age of eighty I discovered that a pinafore is pinned on in front. That I now use the Oxford English Dictionary, not the Imperial, makes me feel a little unfaithful to my mother's memory.

About the age of twelve I gained a scholarship, or bursary, as it was called, to The Royal High School. I wore a black cap with the letters R.H.S. in white. When these letters are made to stand for Royal Horticultural Society, I feel indignant. The school was one of Edinburgh's famous buildings, classical in style and also in its teaching. German, of course, was taught, but we looked down on boys who took German instead of Greek. One could not imagine the Rector, Dr Marshall, teaching German, or, indeed, anything but the classics. And he taught it in an Olympian manner, often with a thunder in his voice that made us boys tremble. When he read his verse translation of Horace's Odes, I always took care to applaud loudly.

Roger Ascham in *The Schoolmaster* thinks it natural that boys should carry away from school a perpetual hatred of their masters. But some of the Royal High School masters I liked! One of them was Mr Cran, a French master, who had a French wife. I almost felt sorry for him when he had to punish me for some offence, perhaps reading a novel in the class; it put him in an embarrassing position. He was a friend of the family and the hand on which he brought down the leather strap might open our house-door to him that night. But Mr Duff, who taught both Latin and Greek, I disliked. He was the chief exponent of the strap; it came down on the palm of the hand with such a resounding smack that it was thought he hardened the leather at a fire. Yet he cordially greeted a visitor to the class, perhaps the Rector, springing to his feet so that his body automatically closed the half-open door of his desk. We knew what was in the desk, a translation! He had so loud a temper that I was surprised to hear of his marriage. They came to live near us, our flats facing each other with their backs, so to speak. I often stood at our kitchen window and watched him washing the dishes. I came to like Mr Duff.

I remember best the English master, Mr White; I even remember that he closed his eyes at Morning Prayers. He was a tall gentleman who wore a surtout, covered of course by his academic gown; he might have been named after his white beard, 'as long as a comet'. He would stroke it thoughtfully when a boy asked such a question as, 'Please,

13

sir, which is correct: he killed the he-goat or he killed the him-goat?' He taught us mainly by mnemonic devices. There have been twelve great English poets, two of them Scots, Burns and Scott; each had seven distinguished contemporaries, so that they formed groups of eight; a mnemonic device was the eight names in a kind of rhythmic couplet:

> Shakespeare Marlowe Lyly Greene:
> Jonson Massinger Chapman Ford.

When we could repeat the twelve couplets, we had a good knowledge of English literature. He also gave us long poems to learn by heart, such as Milton's *L'Allegro*. Pointing to a boy he would say,

> 'On the light fantastic toe,

what is the thirteenth line after that?' If the boy was not good at counting lines with his fingers, he might give the wrong answer. But my heart was not in learning poems by heart, and I lost interest in poetry. I became so addicted to novels that I read them in bed at night, my parents unaware that though the gaslight in my room was out the moon might be shining. I even sent a story to a magazine, but unfortunately each time I used the word 'magic' I spelt it with a j. I little dreamed that the School magazine, *Schola Regia*, would one day review a book of my verse. And what a review! No poet could ever have read anything about himself more gratifying: 'Over thirty years ago Andrew Young won the hundred yards at the School sports for three years in succession.'

Our sports field lay between Holyroodhouse Palace and a brewery; it was a gift of Queen Victoria. There in my first year at school I won a consolation prize. Presented by a well-known Edinburgh bookseller, a former pupil, it was *A Book of Scottish Ballads*. I took it home and after careful consideration returned to the ground to enquire at the pavilion if there had not been some mistake, a silver cup overlooked. At the Holyrood ground I also played rugby and cricket, but it was only in cricket that I excelled. I usually made top score for my team and took many wickets. Unable to get my place in a team of boys of my own age, I chose to play for small boys, by whom I was welcomed. But most of my games were played at Corstorphine, where a new, more spacious field had been acquired by the School. We travelled to and fro by train. Waiting for a train that stopped at Corstorphine, boys were able to buy at the station chocolate at half-price. A halfpenny laid on a railway line and passed over by a fast train became a penny, which could be inserted in a slot-machine.

My physical fitness I must partly have owed to my habit of walking in all weathers to and from the school, about three miles each way. The walk was an education in itself, Edinburgh streets being a kind of visible history. The shortest way was by Princes Street, named after two princes, one of whom became George IV. It was he who, visiting Edinburgh in a kilt, caused Lady Saltoun to remark that as His Majesty's stay was to be short, the more his subjects would see of him the better. As one side of Princes Street has no buildings, Glasgow people say it is only half a street, but it is a case of the half being greater than the whole. The sky-line of the Castle on its rock and the tall tenements of Lawnmarket is engraved on my mind. And there was no large railway hotel to block the view of what few cities possess, a mountain. Scott likened it to 'a couchant lion', and part of it is known as the Lion's Head. It may have had a threatening look, but it was too near the School not to be a standing temptation to its pupils. One day two other boys and I succumbed to the temptation. Unfortunately a master, Mr Turner, put his spy-glass on us, and later we were marched into the Rector's room. He was very wrathful and spoke to us in a thundering voice; then, calming down, he fixed his eyes on me: 'And you with your scholarship deliberately played truant.' Of course, 'deliberately' was silly; I could not have played truant by mistake; but I dislike the word to this day. The others he flogged with the cane, but I escaped! He took away my bursary or, as he called it, scholarship, but that did not matter much, as I gained another before the end of the term. I well deserved it for, not being clever, I must have worked hard for some days before the examination. And nights, too; I seem to remember reading Virgil about one or two o'clock in the morning. If I was punished for my folly, I learned wisdom, never to play truant with other boys and on the Lion's Head.

But my favourite way to school was by the Old Town; it might make me late for Morning Prayers, but attendance was not checked. I started by the Jawbone Walk, so named from an arch made of a whale's bones. It brought me pleasantly across the Meadows to the New University, where my brother studied medicine. Edinburgh's medical skill is said to have been inspired by the foul condition of its streets:

May nane pas throw your principall gaittis
For stink of haddockis and of skattis.

I proceeded by George IV Bridge, from which I looked down in a double sense on the Cowgate, though there had lived the Countess of Galloway, a lady so refined that to visit her next door neighbour she called out her carriage. I reached the High Street to which I looked up in a double sense, its tenements both tall and of a venerable age. There was St. Giles's Church, that like Westminster Abbey was a cathedral for a few years. Perhaps I was more interested in the Law Courts, having an idea that one day I might wear a wig. Sphinxes perched in front were more suggestive of posing riddles than of solving them. Lord Hermand was the Oedipus who solved one riddle: is being drunk a mitigating circumstance in a crime? 'Guid God, if a man will commit murder when he's drunk, what will he not do when he's sober?' From the High Street I reached Princes Street by a railway station named after a novel, Waverley. Or by the North Bridge, where one morning I joined a crowd gazing at an extraordinary spectacle, a car that had broken down. Though it collected a crowd, being the first

16

motor car to enter Edinburgh, its appearance made it seem a poor advertisement for a Newcastle tobacco firm.

But sometimes I made a diversion by the Vennel. It followed the Flodden Wall, raised in fearful haste after the fatal battle. Within its safe shelter the city rose in the sky, tall tenements like streets standing on end. Some were even perched on the Castle Hill, so that their tenants could say,

We that ar heir in hevens glory,
I mene we folk in Paradyis.

I descended to the Grassmarket, cheerful after the hangings. Perhaps it recalled half-hanget Maggie Dickson. Carried away in her coffin, she knocked on the lid and, given a dram of whisky, said she never felt better in her life; she could not be hanged a second time. I climbed to the Lawnmarket, as unlike the Grassmarket as lawn or fine linen is unlike hay. There was Lady Stair's house. When the Earl vainly wooed her as Lady Primrose, he bribed his way into her house and, undressing in the Oratory, stood naked at a window in view of a gathering crowd. This way of wooing has much to commend it, for the compromised lady was won and happily wed. There, too, lived Bailie Macmorran. When High School boys, holding out for longer holidays, barricaded themselves in the school with food and firearms, the Bailie advanced and was shot in the brain. Barricading oneself in a school makes its opposite, playing truant, seem a harmless, even praiseworthy occupation. I am happy to think so, for one of my ways of going to the High School was not to go at all.

Across the road from the School was in those days the Calton Jail; they were more than near neighbours, they had a spiritual affinity. I still have a feeling for Friday, the day before Saturday. As I explain in *A Prospect of Flowers* it was not for pleasure I played truant; what pleasure could there be in having to spend seven hours of the day with nothing to do? It was a matter of principle, though what the principle was I am not clear; perhaps the philosopher Hegel could have elucidated it, for he also played truant from school. When Sir Walter Scott played truant from the High School, his resort was Blackford Hill; but that was too near my new home and I went farther afield. Usually I took the train to Cramond, a village on the Firth of Forth; there I had access to a fine estate owned by the Earl of Rosebery, Dalmeny. Little did I dream, playing truant and trespassing, that the great statesman would one day look up to me, hanging on my words. But so it was; sitting in his pew in Temple Church, he looked up to me standing in the pulpit.

When Tournefort played truant from school, he developed an interest in wild plants; having nothing much else to do at Dalmeny, I developed the same interest. He became the most distinguished botanist of his century, but if I ever knew the difference between a stigma and a stamen I have forgotten. Plants became my favourite hobby-horse for over fifty years. And what a horse it was! climbing mountains and wading into bogs, flying in a plane to the Shetland Isles and the Isles of Scilly. But most of our time we spent ambling along, through woods, over moors and beside streams. So, when my interest in poetry revived, it was natural I should try to write of what I saw and heard, nature poems. These all go back to my truant days at Dalmeny. How much I owe to my kind step-mother, the Royal High School! It was natural she should summon me back to address the boys on a prize-giving day. I gave them some sound advice. As my train drew out of Waverley Station that night, it was mainly of my school-days I was thinking when I repeated, but not in parrot fashion, the Papyngo's words,

Adew, Edinburgh! Thou heych tryumphant toun,
Within quhose boundis rycht blythfull have I bene.

Of course, there were the holidays. For August my mother took us to some seaside place; once it was to Elie, where I gathered garnets on the beach, but usually it was to North Berwick, where we stayed in rooms let by a woman named Lucky Law. My father joined us for week-ends, and we had to accompany him on country walks, perhaps to Tantallon Castle or to North Berwick Law, that falsely looks like a volcano. I remember the clouds of dust raised by horse carriages; it was years before the advent of motor coaches with their notice, 'Please do not speak to the driver.' But most of my time was spent on the beach, where I made companions. With one I fell in love; she was an exotic creature, who spoke in a strange fashion, in fact an English girl. Heaven must have been surprised by a prayer I offered one morning; I prayed that slipping on the rocks she might fall into deep water. Of course, having learnt to swim, I intended to dive in and save her life. For some days nothing happened; then one afternoon going down to the beach I met her coming from it, her dress dripping with water. Though my prayer had not been answered, I felt that at least it had been taken notice of. Later I played golf on the famous links. Though still a stripling, I felt I could play it as well as some of the English gentlemen; in fact, when a London clergyman, Dr Fleming, adopted me as opponent for want of a better, the games were often drawn. Having had the good fortune to be brought up in Edinburgh, not in an English town, I could not remember the time when I could not swing a golf club. Smollett describes the game as he saw it played in Edinburgh. 'In a field called the Links the citizens of Edinburgh divert themselves at a game called Golf, in which they use a curious kind of bats, tipped with horn, and small elastic balls of leather, stuffed with feathers; struck with fierce dexterity from one hole to another, these will fly to an incredible distance.' I had diverted myself on the same links, but with a gutta-percha ball; also on the Braid Hills course, though there I paid two pence for a round. The North Berwick course was more expensive, yet sometimes I paid nothing. I had the habit of rising early in the morning.

In September my father, free from the office of the Insurance Company in which his portrait now hangs, took us for a second holiday. One year it was to Leadhills.

Though it is a poor place with unattractive lead-mines, no-where in Britain could I have spent a more profitable holiday. As instructed by its owner, I placed a long wooden trough in a stream so that it received a gentle flow of water. Then filling a bucket from the bank, I emptied the contents into the trough and, when the water had washed away the sand, I raked the remaining gravel. If a yellow speck caught my eye, I picked it out and put it in a small glass tube. By the time I left Leadhills the tube was half-filled with the same gold as had made the Scottish crown. Many years afterwards it disappeared in a house removal, and with it a tube of pearls my grandfather had fished from the Tay. But I still possess a small tube of garnets.

But usually we went to the Highlands, where we rowed and fished on a loch. At Brig o' Turk my father offered to take me up a mountain, Ben Ledi; perhaps he did, but it was I who took him down and helped to get him to bed with a tumbler of whisky. Mountains became another hobby; I could not see one without considering the best approach to the summit. Apart from the Black Cuillin in Skye and Cir Mhor they were all easily climbed, though Suilven insisted on my going down on hands and knees. My eyesight was more likely to fail than my legs; becoming short-sighted I knew I was in a mist. It might happen suddenly, bright morning changing in a few moments to damp twilight. A mist can be so confusing that you hardly know your right hand from your left. But my trouble with Cir Mhor in Arran was different; attempting to climb it from the Saddle by a trap-dyke, I was so trapped that the rock seemed suitably named trap. I could not return the way I had come, hoisting myself over or wriggling under great blocks of rock; nor could I scale a fifteen-foot cliff. There my bones would be resting had it not been for the unlikely chance that two climbers were on the mountain that morning. I heard their voices and shouted. A face appeared over the cliff and a rope came dangling down. I fastened it tightly under my arms. The climb was not so difficult after all; I could walk up the cliff, my body in a horizontal position.

Mountains and plants went well together; I could ride the two hobby-horses at the same time, for there are over fifty Alpine plants in Britain, one of them, an azalea, the world's smallest flowering shrub. I found them all without difficulty, because I never troubled to look for them; a friend who knew I did not dig up and collect rare plants gave me secret and intimate directions. So if Ben Lui was my first mountain, my last was about sixty years later: the higher Slioch. I liked being alone on a mountain; it seemed the proper thing; but I came to learn that there could be a richer loneliness with a companion, one closer than a brother. She was a better climber than I was. I remember that on Tryfan she made straight for the summit on cautious hands and knees, while I made a safe detour. On Cader Idris she even climbed beyond the summit. A terrific gale was blowing and one gust lifted her light figure in the air. Fortunately she fell, not on the rock, but on a patch of grass. I tell our friends how in the course of a twenty-seven-mile walk she climbed two mountains, both higher than Snowdon; but she always spoils the story by pointing out that there is not a deep dip between Cairngorm and Ben Macdhui.

At the age of eighteen I went to Edinburgh University, taking the Arts Course, on which I spent five years instead of the customary three. That allowed me time for my own education. I read widely, from Lao-tze to Baudelaire; I remember 'Requite hatred with good' and also 'cats that languish on pianos and sob like women, with hoarse sweet voices'. I took great interest in the Fine Art class, gaining a prize, fifteen pounds, which supplemented by my father allowed me to spend half a year in the Latin Quarter of Paris, continuing my study. In the other classes I took less interest; I have even forgotten what they all were. Of course, there was Latin and Greek, but I might have said with Allan Ramsay that I was none the worse in not knowing these languages than Virgil and Homer were in not knowing Scots. I was not too proud to seek help from a translation like Mr Duff. And there was English literature. Professor Saintsbury must have been one of the world's greatest readers; it was popularly reported that in reading a book he read two lines at a time, if not three. The last time I saw him was in Bath; passing a house I caught sight of him through a window; his hand was stretched towards a bookcase. I should have liked to call; we might have talked about Elgin, where according to my father he had been a schoolmaster. Or I could have told him that I did not pay much attention to his lectures; that might have pleased him, for I should have explained it was because I attached much more importance to his books. Of the Logic and Metaphysics class I best recall an examination paper, with which I found some difficulty; I tried to put things right by a quotation. Professor Pringle-Pattison must have stroked his beard thoughtfully like Mr White when he read,

> How charming is divine philosophy!
> Not harsh and crabbed as dull fools suppose,
> But musical as is Apollo's lute.

I look back on examinations as I look back on mountain mists, wondering how I came through them all; they seem less to have been passed than by-passed. But Edinburgh University was to me a true Alma Mater, Kind Mother. Speaking at a dinner on behalf of those on whom honorary degrees were being conferred, I expressed my own warm feeling at returning after long years to my Alma Mater; I quoted Sappho, very suitably in the learned company: 'Hesperus, bringer of all things the bright dawn scattered, thou bringest the sheep, thou bringest the goat, thou bringest the child to its mother'.

Though like Queen Victoria I was 'so attached to the dear, dear Highlands', I became in my student days even more attached to the Border Country. Hills with soft-flowing lines, birches with their hair hanging over their heads, wide valleys with the plaintive sound of running water, no doubt these things gave it a pensive beauty. Yet what attracted me was in stark contrast, bastel-houses, pele-towers and strange castles like the two Fatlips, one on Minto, the other on Tinto. I even looked at dull Jedburgh prison, for it replaced the castle where Alexander III had his interview with the dancing skeleton. What drew me to Melrose Abbey was not the carved foliage, but Michael Scot's tomb. Though it was only the reputed tomb, that he had not found a watery grave made me somehow feel it was the real tomb. When the Wizard conjured up a demon in the form of a horse and rode across the sea to France, 'What do the old women of Scotland say at bed-time?' asked the horse. Had he said 'The Lord's Prayer', the horse would have vanished, leaving him to drown. He told the horse not to talk.

Among the books I possessed was one precious volume, the consolation prize, *A Book of Scottish Ballads*. Someone said that ballads were lame on their metrical feet, but with me they went well. I appreciated them more than Sir Philip Sidney who said, 'I never heard the olde song of *Percy* and *Douglas*, that I found not my heart mooved more than with a Trumpet', but goes on, 'what would it not worke trymmed in the gorgeous eloquence of Pindar?' It would work disaster. The nature of the ballads is to be simple:

> 'My lover's blood is on thy spear.
> How canst thou bid me love thee?'

They cannot be too simple to be moving:

> I canna look on that bonnie face,
> As it lies in the grass.

In those romantic years the Border Country with its ballads worked on me with a magic.

> O sweet and far from cliff and scar
> The horns of Elfland faintly blowing;

yet not faintly if I was near the Eildon Hills, where True Thomas followed the Faerie Queen into Elfland.

I was religiously brought up; one of my earliest recollections is of kneeling at my father's knees and repeating after him the Lord's Prayer. I also remember being laid across his knees. But I was naturally religious; when another little boy pointed out to me that 'God' was 'dog' spelt the other way round, I received a great shock. At any time I might have said with Samuel Butler, 'to be at all is to be religious, more or less'. Yet I hesitated a long time before deciding to enter the Church; the idea of the Law was still in my mind; it was this hesitation that kept me five years at the university. What helped me to decide in the end was the case of my father. He had somehow assumed I would become a minister. The headmaster predicted I should one day stand in the pulpit! Meanwhile my brother had gone as a doctor to Singapore; he wrote home each week, till suddenly the letters ceased. That was the end; all that my father could learn was that he had disappeared. When I set out for Paris some months later, intending to stay in London with my uncle on the way, my father's parting words were, 'keep your eyes open for David'. So hopeless a request was deeply pathetic. Later in Paris, when a Frenchman asked about my future profession, I replied, 'I mean to be a minister'. I remember the incident because he looked surprised; he thought I meant a Minister of State.

For four years I attended a theological college. My difficulty was with Hebrew; it has no vowels in its alphabet, the vowel sounds indicated by small marks called points. I had good eyesight when I gathered garnets and gold; it must have sadly deteriorated, for when I showed a Hebrew Bible to an eye-specialist, a friend of the family, he pronounced my eyesight unfit to study the language. He wrote accordingly to the Senatus, and I was exempted. The Senatus was very kind. Yet I became very friendly with Professor Paterson; perhaps it was because he had no difficulty in teaching me Hebrew! When I was called to

Temple Church, I invited him for the Induction. In his sermon he compared me with Moses; at least, he spoke of the call which both of us received. Professor Mackintosh was also kind; he allowed me on Fridays to leave the theology class a quarter of an hour before the end to catch the one o'clock train to Glasgow. I doubt if he ever quite understood the nature of my engagement; I could not have entered on a more serious engagement. It was on a Friday afternoon my mountaineering companion and I climbed Ben Lomond.

Yet at the New College I had another difficulty. Students were expected to take occasional services, especially in a small country church; my difficulty was the sermon. Travelling in a train on a Saturday evening, I longed for some disaster to happen, which would prevent my standing in the pulpit next day. I was nervous in the pulpit, and not without reason. On one occasion I noticed a face beaming up at me; I saw what I had done; to illustrate St Paul's humility I had quoted two of his sayings, 'I am the chief of sinners' and 'By the grace of God I am what I am'. I little dreamed that I should ever broadcast the Christmas morning sermon, for, of course, there was no broadcasting in those days.

While I benefited greatly from the professors' lectures and the seminars they held, I benefited more from my talks with two of my fellow-students, John and Donald Baillie; both became professors of theology, John with a European reputation. In some of our evening talks we were joined by John Laird, who became a professor of philosophy. Calling on me one morning John Baillie looked around the room in wonder and said in an awed voice, 'Was this where we talked last night?' Even in those days I was frightened by his learning; later he told me he was tired of receiving honorary degrees from foreign universities. But Donald had the sharper mind. He used often to say, 'But what do these words mean? Anything?' He was already in a way a linguistic philosopher, though he would not have based his philosophy on anything so utilitarian in its origin and use as language. And it was he who most often pointed out to me that I was no philosopher, I who had read Sir William Hamilton's *Lectures on Metaphysics* before I left school. Even in those days I was a Berkeleian.

In my boyhood days it was not uncommon for me to have a strange experience. It might happen anywhere, but I remember it best at Dalmeny, when I was playing truant. Suddenly the world around me lost its material look;

> objects of themselves
> Melted away to their own images,
> An insubstantial world.

Trees, bushes, fields, rocks, the seashore,

> Nothing was changed, but all was visionary,
> And I was in a waking dream.

I was looking at a strange world, yet with no sense of surprise. Sometimes I could induce the experience by saying, 'I see what I am seeing', words that suggest it was the world in its true nature I was viewing, or so I felt. It was less from reading Berkeley than from looking back on that boyhood experience that I became a Berkeleian. Of course, as Donald Baillie pointed out, I was no philosopher.

With that experience behind me perhaps it was natural I should supplement my theological studies with an interest in mystic writings. Certainly Meister Eckhart, Doctor of Theology, was a change from my New College professors: 'I do not thank God for loving me, because He cannot help it'; 'To say God is good is as incorrect as to say white is black'. He was charged with heresy for saying he created the universe with his little finger. Perhaps I preferred his disciple, Jan Ruysbroek, who for his poetry alone might have deserved the title, The Admirable. He, too, said that God was not good, but added, 'He is the principle of Goodness'. But the writers to whom I was most drawn were Spanish. With the Blessed St. Teresa I had something in common, her favourite book as a girl had been mine as a boy, *Amadis of Gaul*. And she was a woman

of great charm; she hurried through her meals to be first
at the kitchen sink; 'God', she said, 'walks among the pots
and pans'. With 'my little Seneca', as she called him, the
learned St John of the Cross, I had also something in
common, a love of mountains; he climbed them on Satur-
days, as I sometimes did myself, having spent Friday night
in Glasgow. He, too, had great charm; when he spoke of
holy things at the refectory table, 'he made us all laugh'; on
Christmas Day he danced with a little statue of Jesus in his
arms. Perhaps I had something in common with Richard
Rolle of Hampole; he ran away from Oxford at the age of
nineteen, and, when he became a hermit, he did not stay
in his cell as the regulation was. At our evening talks I
tried to interest my fellow-students in these writers, des-
cribing their flights, illuminations and visions of God in a
point, but they preferred the German theologians. Perhaps
now they are interested:

> They are all gone into the world of light!

Certainly after my own death and burial I maintained my
interest. *Out of the World and Back* tells how, finding myself in another world, I wondered,

> was I near the Magnetic Mountain,
> Climbed by those saints who,
> wounded with love's arrow,
> Had sought for healing at their Hunter's wounds;

I even wondered if I should ever myself attain

> the Dark Silence,
> Where all lovers lose themselves.

During my New College days I began to wander farther
afield than the Border Country. I recall the thrill with
which, having crossed the Tweed from Berwick, I first set
foot on English soil. I had forgotten that Berwick was in
England! But it was not country or people that caused me
to make frequent journeys across the border; starting with
Carlisle and Durham, I began collecting cathedrals as I
had once collected postage stamps. The stamps are gone,

but the faded cathedrals remain in an old-fashioned post-card album. Ely's lantern tower, York's Five Sisters, Lincoln's Angel Choir, Canterbury's Bell Harry, Wells's chapter-house, Salisbury's spire and the fan-vaulting of Gloucester's cloisters, these, unmatched anywhere in their kind, were the Seven Wonders of England. Yet the parish churches became more endearing.

> Stone foliage
> Showed me the spring in winter at West Walton;
> Angels smiled down, as they spread their wooden wings
> To fly off with Knapton's roof.

Scotland is fortunate in having on its doorstep England, a country richer for its size in parish churches than any other in Christendom. They are more individual than French churches, which look like young cathedrals. Yet they fit in with the landscape, or, rather, the landscape fits in with them, for they are older than the pattern of fields, hedges and coppices. They take you far into the past; the walk by the water-meadows to Saxon Deerhurst may take only half an hour, yet you wander back through a thousand years. *Out of the World and Back* tells how, conscious of a somewhat chill reception in the other world, I warmed myself with their memories,

> from Norman naves,
> Monsters that stand on elephantine legs
> Tame at the altar, to the little churches
> With scarcely room for God.

Anglican churches do more than fit in with a landscape; they complete it or, at least, add a spiritual value. A tower with its clock may tell the time, but it is time's adversary; it stands for what is eternal, a strong tower against the enemy. So my interest in churches was not purely architectural. And there was something more; I was drawn to them by the Anglican ritual. I even cast my eye on rich vestments, though I have found the best time to pray is immediately after a bath, a naked state very suited to a

28

prayer. But I put the idea of entering the Anglican Communion out of my mind, and I kept it out during the years I was minister of Temple Church and later and longer of a church in Hove. I was considering my father; he was more than a Presbyterian, an Original Seceder.

That my father was reconciled to the step I took in the end was largely due to a stranger I met in a train. I was travelling from London to Edinburgh and he was the only other occupant of the compartment. Each time I raised my eyes from my book he took the opportunity to talk. I became strangely interested in his talk. He seemed to know who I was, as though he had seen my photograph and read about me in some paper. I was curious about him, but any tentative enquiries I made he put off with a beaming smile. When I saw him next morning, he was standing before the altar of an episcopal church in Edinburgh, waiting for the bride, my sister Margaret. That my father had a son-in-law who was an Anglican, and also a daughter who had become one, reconciled him to my entering the Anglican Communion. It seems a pity he did not live to learn that I became a Canon of Chichester Cathedral a few years after my Confirmation.

While I was still at the New College, my father paid sixteen pounds to have published a book of poems, *Songs of Night*. I believe it begins:

> Go now, my song
> Let your wing be strong,
> Fly and dart and dip
> With a chip, chip;
> A wren among the thorn
> Of the world's scorn,
> Let not courage fail
> Your upturned tail.

Fortunately I cannot quote more, as I do not possess a copy of the book.

As apart from religion poetry was my chief interest, I have seen the generations of poets rise and fall. Lewis

Carroll gave good advice for writing prose, 'Look after the sense and the sounds will look after themselves'; Swinburne did the opposite in writing verse. We were carried away by his mellifluous music, though perhaps not prepared to change in a trice

> The lilies and languors of virtue
> For the roses and raptures of vice.

The Decadents were different:

> I am so tired of holly sprays
> And weary of the bright box tree.

But they, too, affected sounds; Dowson's favourite line was

> The viol, the violet and the vine.

The Georgians brought new life into poetry. Some of them I knew, though not the one I most admired, Edward Thomas. But I knew his mother, whom I used to visit in a boarding-house in Brighton. Though the Georgians set a new fashion, to some young poets they may seem as old-fashioned as Georgian houses. What causes the flow and ebb of popularity is what the wise Ulysses describes as the one touch of nature that makes the whole world kin, the love of novelty. Mercutio, another Shakespeare character, might be thinking of poets and their readers when he speaks of those 'who stand so much on the new form that they cannot sit on the old bench'. The love of novelty is old; 'Old wine, new songs', cries Pindar, and Homer makes Odysseus tell his son what the young man probably knew better than his father, 'the minstrels' songs men love most are the new songs'. It makes judgements on contemporary poets likely to be mistaken. 'Nothing in our age is more preposterous than the current judgement upon poetry and poets'; if Ben Jonson could say that of his great Elizabethan age, it is likely to be true of this Elizabethan age. As for a poet's opinion of himself, he is, of course, his own contemporary!

But turning from poets to myself, I must not omit the outstanding memory of my early days. It was recalled to me in a singular way when my mountaineering companion and I—she is a relation by marriage!—travelled by night train to Scotland. As we sat in the refreshment room before joining the train, a man entered, looked at my companion and looked again. Then, sitting with a glass of beer, he continued to look in spite of my raised eyebrows. It seemed mysterious, and when later, standing by myself in the corridor of the train, I saw him slowly approach, I was a little apprehensive. I thought he might be insane, but he was the sanest man I ever met. What he said was, 'You must have wondered at my looking at the lady in the refreshment room'. I replied that I was surprised. 'But I could not help it,' he explained; 'she was very beautiful'. That is a memory of my early days, and of days much later, even recent, for the incident occurred the year I climbed, this time alone, Slioch.

THE NEW POLY-OLBION

FOREWORD

Poly-Olbion means 'very happy', the reference being to Albion. Camden says that if the most Omnipotent had fashioned the world as a ring instead of as a globe, Britain would be its only gem; Drayton, the poet of *Poly-Olbion*, would have agreed. But it was from his native Warwickshire he received his inspiration:

> Fayre *Arden*, thou my *Tempe* art alone,
> And thou, sweet *Ankor*, art my *Helicon*.

He forgot, like other poets, that Helicon is a hill, not a river. Perhaps rivers were running too much in his head, the poem being mainly taken up with their love affairs. If the River Tyne could see *The New Poly-Olbion*, it might exclaim as in Drayton's poem, 'Good Lord!'

Some of these pieces have borrowed material from a book now safely out of print, *A Prospect of Britain*. Three have appeared in a periodical that encourages experiments in poetry, *Priapus*.

THE THAMES

THE STRIPLING THAMES is like a poor student of the old days on his way to Oxford. Though a stripling, it needs an effort to move at all,

> The level ground a breathless hill.

Pollard willows watch it with thoughtful heads; it is no stripling in a flood. The boatman finds it friendly, the banks coming close to offer bunches of willowherb and purple loosestrife. At Oxford it is of three minds how to proceed. It breaks up and there are three striplings; they suit a city,

> Where academic gowns flap like the wings
> Of half-fledged blackbirds that attempt to fly.

It goes down from Oxford with an air of importance. Though tributaries are the opposite of offspring, they help it to play the part, Father Thames. It can spare enough of itself to form shadowy backwaters, lit by happy, lazy lights. Tall lines of Lombardy poplars stand stiff as sentinels, but casting shaky shadows on the water; weeping willows brush lawns with their trailing skirts; cedars spread shelves of flat foliage.

> O, art thou sighing for Lebanon,
> Dark Cedar?

The sigh is of contentment with the Thames Valley.

It passes Windsor with a gentle sweep, a river's nearest approach to a bow. It is busy with traffic, water in the locks rising and falling in tides of ten minutes. Yet it finds time to make charming water-colours of bungalows and boat-houses. It is the river of poets, though few suspend the dashing oar to sigh and say,

> In yonder Grave a Druid lies.

36

It approaches London with a portly dignity, the poor Oxford student become an alderman. But embankments reduce it from river to water-way, agitated by tides. If I were to send

> my supremest kiss
> To thee, my silver-footed Thamasis,

I should not address the letter to London. My supremest kiss I should send to Sonning or Sutton Courteney, or even to both.

IN ST. PAUL'S CATHEDRAL

WALKING ALONG the choir aisle, I came face to face with the Dean. His eyes were closed, but I thought he gave me a quick glance. He was garbed as on the day he had his picture drawn, his naked body in a shroud with only the face exposed. The picture was intended to be copied in a monument, and the figure I saw is thought to be the monument, which had escaped the Great Fire; but something told me I was seeing the Dean himself, petrified, not for looking back like Lot's wife, but for looking forward, playing the part of a corpse. The figure showed stains of fire, but they were the stains, not of the Great Fire, but of a greater, Purgatory. So now John Donne was in Heaven. 'There we shall all be children of one Quire, and never grow lazie'; in Heaven he was not a Dean, but a well-behaved choir-boy. As a young man he had seen an angel in the sign of the Mermaid Tavern, now he beheld real angels. Did he delight them with his wit? Did he repeat his pun about angels, heavenly beings and gold coins, warning them that some angels could be put on the fire and melted down? Did they call him Jack? Meanwhile his body, which had become its own monument, was still in the cathedral, in the choir aisle, never to return to his great-grand-mother, Dust. His desire had been to die in the pulpit; he had done better, become himself a sermon. How foolishly was a famous Shakespeare passage emended to, 'sermons in books, stones in the running brooks'. 'Sermons in stones' is correct; here was the proof, the most eloquent sermon ever preached in St Paul's.

CHELSEA PHYSIC GARDEN

THOUGH IT WAS a chill March morning, the Physic Garden was ablaze with plants. Happy were the men who tended them, making their beds;

> here every man
> Was his own Patient and Physician.

There was goutweed, a singularly virtuous plant, for it cures gout and also by its other name, bishop's-weed, warns certain persons of their bibulous habits. There was yarrow, a panacea; growing in a graveyard it is a reproach to the dead. And saffron crocus; a crocodile, coming out of the Thames and crossing the road to the garden, would be dismayed; only when it sees the saffron crocus are its tears genuine; even the name, crocodile or crocus-dreader, speaks of the reptile's antipathy to the life-saving plant. There were many others; Hampstead Heath could have supplied a score of medicinal herbs; in *Poly-Olbion* it claims

> in simples to have skill
> and therefore by desert to be the noblest Hill.

But I missed mandrake, the mandragora that could have medicined Othello to a sweet sleep. It is so full of sleep itself that it groans on being dragged from its bed. John Donne in love wished himself a mandrake to groan. Perhaps the plant was still fast asleep, for the others were as yet hardly awake; only with their virtues was the Physic Garden ablaze.

A QUAKER COURTSHIP

WHEN *Poly-Olbion* speaks of the Chilterns as 'mountain-ously high', it is making mountains of molehills. You are in a friendly country; cottages, fitting into the landscape, seem at home; villages form triangles, their windows glancing at each other across a pond; town halls, far from standing on their dignity, stand across a main street to bid you welcome. The beechwoods' sighing has a human sound; when you enter, tall trees curtsey and dead leaves rush to kiss your feet. This amiable country seems suited to a Quaker courting a Quakeress and sleeping with her in a graveyard.

One wonders how William Penn courted Guli. He could not remove his hat; it was not to her he said his prayers. Nor could he say 'you', 'a corrupt way of speaking in the plural to a single person'; yet 'thou' was disrespectful; to 'thou' a man was Sir Toby Belch's way of picking a quarrel. Nor could he give her presents, 'those vulgar ways of courtship'; Guli's mother had no wedding ring. But perhaps little courtship was needed. Thomas Ellwood considered Guli 'in all respects a very desirable Woman'; he was 'not so devoid of Natural Heat, as not to feel some Sparklings of Desire'; as he had shared her perambulator, pushed by a footman, he might share her bed; but he was content with the consolation prize, Mary Ellis. 'William was the one.' He still admits it publicly in his tombstone at Jordans, for while William and Guli sleep side by side, he lies a little way behind. The three sleep very peacefully under the dumb turf, for in earth they neither marry nor are given in marriage.

WOTTON

'Wood-born, as I am': Evelyn meant, not that he was stupid, but that his birthplace was Wotton, House-by-the-Wood. It is also by the Tillingbourne, a stream that talks all day of its charm, eloquent at the waterfall. It lies at the foot of Leith Hill, which Evelyn may not have admired; for him the Alps looked like piled-up sweepings from the levelled Lombardy Plain. A mountain could not compare with a tree.

But 'wood-born' suggests something about Evelyn himself:
if he could not see

> A noble spirit in a hill,

he could feel

> A human touch about a tree.

It might be a cold feeling; a birch was despicable and an elder both despicable and vulgar. But usually it was a warm feeling; an oak was a goodly stick and an arboreous temple. He so praised the horse-chestnut that all over England it lights its Christmas candles in May. There was no more glorious sight under heaven than his own holly-hedge. Yet the Russian Czar, Peter the Great, delighted in being driven through it in a wheelbarrow! Sayes Court deserved a better tenant.

Evelyn speaks of other tree-lovers, Passienus Crispus, who fell in love with a beech, giving its roots wine and sleeping in its shade, and Xerxes, who halted an army to call a plane his mistress and deck it with jewels. He also quotes with approval the philosophers' dictum, *Homo est planta inversa*, but changing *planta* to *arbor*. He does not say, however, which he considered upside down, tree or man. Aristotle thought it was the tree with its mouth to the ground; perhaps Evelyn thought it was man, his head in the air.

PEVENSEY

Pevensey stood by a wide lagoon, where vessels of the British fleet, *classis Britannica*, rode at anchor, hulls and rigging painted sea-green and sailors garbed in the same colour. But the sea began to withdraw, leaving a narrow estuary, the Haven. Freemen of Pevensey had the right to be drowned in the Haven instead of being hanged, but its main use was to keep alive the sea-port. Merry Andrew, a native, was not jesting when he compared Pevensey with Portsmouth. Now sheep are in the place of ships, the sea a mile away.

When I went down to Pevensey Bay, I half-expected to see William the Conqueror lying on the beach. Anything was possible in the queer evening light, and he had landed from the bay, falling on his face. All I saw was a lonely figure that crouched by the water's edge, offering a prayer to Neptune. A heavy wave tumbled over itself and rushed up the stony beach to bid me welcome; when I gave it the cold shoulder, it withdrew with an ugly snarl. It was still the same sea, not to be trusted. I said to myself,

> With waves that up the shingle shoot
> In haste to lick my foot
> How false and fawning is the sea,
> Like him who crouches on bent knee,
> Waiting till bass or ling too late
> Discovers the sly bait.

As the incoming tide sent waves farther up the beach, the sea became more determined to lick my foot; but I was not to be flattered. I grew so accustomed to its advances, effusive but idle, that I found myself saying,

> Now as I walk away
> Across the flats of Pevensey Bay,

My footsteps on the desert beach
Keeping up a stony speech,
I fear the sea, leaving the shore,
Follows my heel to dog me to my door.

KINGLEY VALE

OTHER AGED YEWS are numinous, as the Crowhurst yew in Surrey and the Crowhurst yew in Sussex, and the Fortingall yew, in whose shade Pontius Pilate played as a boy, his father in command of the Roman camp. *Poly-Olbion* tells how the yew in which the priest hid the virgin's head became so famous as a shrine that the village, Horton, changed its name,

> *Halifax* since nam'd, which in the Northern tongue
> Is *Holy hair*.

But the Kingley Vale yews! *numen inest.*

The grove was screened from profane eyes by trees, withered clematis bines dangling from their boughs over blossoming gorse,

> That lay like gold unguarded
> By dragons that hung dead.

As I passed through a gap, twilight changed to night. Moving about in the dark, cautious as a cat, I acquired a cat's eyes. I made out the uncertain shapes of three or four yews that appeared to form a temple. I touched a huge bough, almost a tree itself, which sloped from the trunk's black mass to plunge into the earth; my hand paused on it, sharing its thousand years. Moving on,

> Watched by a single star,
> A fitful fiery Lucifer,

I pushed my way through the bushes that tried to hold me back into another temple. It appeared to be more spacious than the first, and more heathenish. Five or six yews, each an octopus, held out wild arms heavy on the air or striking the ground. Tumbling about and intercepting one another, these boughs were possessed by a demonic power not proper to trees. There was the secret of the weird wood!

44

Driving out the dryads, a legion of evil spirits had seized the grove and were giving this fiendish display. It was no place of worship. I should have been frightened, had it not been so woodenly insane. The numinous was overdone in Kingley Vale.

GRAND AVENUE

SAVERNAKE FOREST has Methuselahs, though some
hardly behave as such,

> old wrinkled trees
> Struck by sunbeams in umbered shades
> Ogling each other with gay oeillades.

The Duke's Vaunt boasts of a concert it gave, violin, haut-
boy and bassoon in its hollow trunk; Big-bellied Oak, far
from hollow yet, stands shamelessly by a public road.
Though wolf and boar are gone, you expect to see the
animal engraved on the Warder's horn, the unicorn.

When Savernake ceased to be a royal demesne, to a new
owner it appeared old-fashioned,

> a foreste
> With knotty knarry bareyn trees;

he could not see the wood for the trees. An admirer of
Georgian architecture, he planned a more formal style of
forest, its chief feature Grand Avenue. But trees, unlike
houses, have the habit of growing up, and what he de-
signed to be Georgian proved to be Gothic. Coming from
Salisbury Cathedral to Grand Avenue, you feel you are
back in the cathedral, driving your car down its Early
English nave. Perhaps you are in the truer cathedral.
Though the beeches are old for beeches and there are
ominous gaps in their rows, Grand Avenue may outlast
Salisbury Cathedral. Its upper tower and spire, added as a
weighty afterthought, may collapse at any moment; the
collapse has been expected for centuries. No disaster need
befall Grand Avenue, young trees already in the gaps. You
are in a living cathedral, dedicated to the animal with the
one horn, the unicorn, emblem of Christ.

BREAMORE MAZE

DAEDALUS lost himself in his own labyrinth. Turf-mazes are different; though Gonzolo speaks of their forth-rights and meanders, they are not puzzles; a child could go straight to the centre, except that he would go in circles. Only their purpose is puzzling. The Julian's Bowers and Troy Towns, named after Iulus and the game in which he led the bashful boys, the Troy game, may have invited the British swain

> to take his Reed, and chant his Layes,
> And nimbly run the windings of the Maze.

The maze on St. Catherine's Hill, near ecclesiastical Winchester, may have invited sinners to crawl its course, a form of penance. The Breamore maze may be older than the Saxon church and a ritual dancing-floor. The one thing certain is that mazes were the haunt of fairies. When Titania says to Oberon,

> the quaint mazes in the wanton green,
> For lack of tread are undistinguishable,

she is thinking of them as deserted by the British swain, not by fairies, too light-footed to leave tracks. They might still haunt Breamore maze, a mizmase. It is lonely, strangely secluded by trees, and queer, even startling, the ground with its ridges and hollows tossing like a restless sea. But treading its tiny thoroughfares, I met no traffic, not even Queen Mab's wagon,

> Made by the joiner squirrel or old grub,
> Time out o' mind, the fairies' coach-makers.

The case was clear; poets felt they had to adopt a patronizing attitude to fairies, and that was more than they could stand.

The poets, knowing what the public wants,
Writing of fairies, drove them from their haunts.

THE
UFFINGTON WHITE HORSE

ENGLAND'S TURF, the natural element in which it excels, has bred famous horses not connected with the Turf. The Edgehill White Horse,

> Tysoe's wondrous theme, the Martial Horse,
> Carv'd on the yielding turf,

now lies under the unyielding turf, having left only a name, the Vale of the Red Horse; but the Westbury White Horse is soon to celebrate its tricentenary. Lying on a steep slope, it stands almost upright. Yet it has a dejected look; it is not like the horses trained on the downs,

> that with loud hooves
> Print on the turf their lucky grooves;

you would not back it for a winner. It is the sire of the Wiltshire stud and, so far-reaching its fame, it may have sired the Mormond White Horse and even—who knows? —the Mormond Stag.

These horses have a remote ancestor, as alive as ever he was, in the Uffington White Horse,

> brave Pegasian Steed,
> The wonder of the West, exalted to the Skyes.

It has not passed on a family likeness, for while the Wiltshire horses look equine, it has been taken for the dragon slain by St. George. Iron Age coins, however, show horses of the kind. It is so agile a creature that as it races along the downs, the low curve of its back fits in with their flowing lines. This is the more remarkable, as two of its legs have dropped off. Perhaps it has also lost a shoe, for it appears to be making its way to Wayland Smith's Cave, where it is said to have been shod. Though it has been running so long, it is still near the Manger, the combe out of which it bounded, so near that the race seems hardly to have begun. It makes you feel you are back in the Iron Age.

COLD COTSWOLDS

CROCUSES in gardens were awake, stretching themselves and yawning; if daffodils are the spring's trumpets, as poets tell us, every garden had its brass band; the flowers even trespassed on public roads. But it was still winter on the wolds; the long lines of beeches were shamelessly naked, shivering in a wind you could see; even violets shivered in their purple hoods. There were no primroses, for those sweet Infantas of the year keep off the cold wolds. I felt coldly towards them myself. But I warmed myself with old memories, of chambered barrows, from the Whispering Knights, a denuded skeleton, to Hetty Pegler's Tump, so far from a skeleton that Hetty looks plump, even pregnant. And with memories of buildings in the Tudor tradition, from manor-houses with an ambiguity as to what they are, domestic or ecclesiastical, to small houses that have a dignity that makes you feel inferior to their owners; the Royal Family could live in Chipping Campden's alms-houses.

But the cold Cotswolds added a new memory. Driving over the Edge in twilight, I saw what was apocalyptic. Dark cloud shadowed the sky and the Severn Valley lay in deep shade, but between cloud and shadow burned a sunset, a long sea of fire. There, if anywhere, were 'the flaming ramparts of the world'. Or was I seeing farther, not a sunset, but a sunrise on another world? No, it was too lurid; it was a reflection from some infernal region. And I was hastening down to it, leaving not only the Cotswolds, but the earth itself. Drawing closer to my companion, the sharer of old memories, I said silently,

> You have so much forgiven,
> Forgive me this or that, or Hell or Heaven.

MALVERN HILLS

THE MALVERNS might be a mountain range that migrated from Wales; contrary to the habit of English hills they stretch north and south, and Worcestershire Beacon looks every inch a mountain, though not every foot. Some mountains have bad neighbours, interrupting their views; the Beacon is one of England's best observatories. The plain that spreads for miles was Piers Plowman's half-acre. In Langland's time it was mostly woodland; now the only woods are moving cloud-shadows. Centuries of cultivation have made it more intensely Piers Plowman's half-acre, Piers being the English yeoman.

But Piers in the poem is more; though he has a daughter, Behave-well-or-thy-mother-will-give-thee-a-beating, he is also a cleric. Lady Holy Church has taught him such truths as,

Chastity without charity   shall be chained in Hell.

He has four great oxen to plough with, Matthew, Mark, Luke and John, and four fine horses, Augustine, Ambrose, Gregory and Jerome, to harrow in their wake, destroying ill weeds like restharrow. When Jesus rode into Jerusalem to joust with the foul Fiend and lose His life for His Lady, yet in the end to harrow Hell, it was with Piers' armour and human nature,

His helmet and his hauberk   *humana natura*.

So the half-acre has produced more than cider apples and perry pears, three cathedrals and many monastic buildings, one the mighty Tewkesbury Abbey. With, 'Will, sleepest thou?' Lady Holy Church pointed out the wonderful vision to Langland. Failing that Lady there is an indicator on the Beacon.

BATH AND WELLS

THOUGH BOTH TOWNS have watery names—the Bishop
of Bath and Wells must be an amphibian—they could not
be more unlike. They are separated by more than the
Mendips; they are streets apart. And they have little in
common; while Bath is a popular spa, Wells has only a
bishop's tomb in the cathedral reputed to cure toothache.
Yet Bath owes much to a Dean of Wells, Doctor Turner,
the Father of English Botany. He wrote a treatise so com-
mending its waters that the main road from London to the
West is called the Bath Road. He was a peculiar Dean; he
refused to wear a surplice and trained his dog to snatch off
the Bishop's square cap; 'he contemneth all Bishopps and
calleth them white coats, typpett gentlemen.' Yet he
might not have approved of the new spa; 'to see Old Men
and Women; Boyes and Girles, one with another, peepe
up in their Caps, and appeare so nakedly, and fearefully,
would putt one in mind of the Resurrection'.

That was not a comfortable thought. The bathers might
not have used the prayers written for them by the saintly
Bishop Ken. It was of bathers in the baths, not in the
moat of the Bishop's Palace, that young Simkin wrote
home to his mother,

> 'Twas a glorious sight to see the fair sex
> All wading with gentlemen up to their necks.

No doubt, Bath has an Abbey, but its storied urns and
animated busts speak less of heaven than of earth; the nave
of Wells Cathedral is of heavenly inspiration, the first pure
Gothic in England, if not in Europe. Bath has statues to
men like Beau Nash, a professional gambler; on the west
front of Wells are statues of more than three hundred
saints. No place is so haunted by ghosts as Bath; all the
pilgrims to St Andrew's shrine are in heaven with the
Bishop and the—— But one wonders about the Dean.

What can be his attitude to the angels, even to the arch-angels? Are they, too, white coats, typpett gentlemen? It would be interesting to learn; I am glad that I lived in Wells, and in the Vicars' Close.

GLASTONBURY

THE ABBOT'S KITCHEN looks like a banqueting-hall; perhaps it was one, the abbot's guests, even kings and queens, given their meals in the kitchen. The Abbey is in sad contrast, its floor mostly turf and ruined walls looking too pathetic to be stone. Its greatness is now only in great names, St Patrick, St Dunstan, and above all, Joseph of Arimathea.

To the Benedictine monks Joseph was a tin-master. On one of his visits to Cornwall, the world's chief source of tin, he took with him the boy Jesus. Perhaps the boy had read in Caesar that Britons painted their bodies with woad and, seeing no painted people in Cornwall, he persuaded Joseph to take him to Glastonbury or Woadtown. There he pointed out the likeness of Glastonbury Tor to Mount Tabor. The likeness remained in Joseph's mind, and he returned to Glastonbury to end his days. His staff he planted in a hill, Weary-all, where it took root and grew to be a shrub. While other shrubs bloom at Easter, the Glastonbury Thorn commemorates our Lord's nativity. He also planted in a hill the Holy Grail, a vessel used by our Lord at the Last Supper.

But another story arose. Joseph was not a tin-master but a soldier who faithfully served Pilate for seven years and after the crucifixion put a cross on his shield and became the Good Soldier. Through him the Grail passed into the possession of the rich King Fisherman, who kept it in a castle encompassed by a river that rose in the Earthly Paradise. There it was seen by Percival, related to Joseph by his mother, the Widow Lady. It was seen by other knights, two of them Joseph's descendants, Lancelot of the Lake and Galahad, 'the best knight that ever was since God was born'. But the Grail has not gone from Glastonbury any more than the Glastonbury Thorn which still keeps Christmas in the Abbey grounds. What the knights saw was a chalice; according to Tennyson

> the cup itself, from which our Lord
> Drank at the last sad supper.

The Holy Grail is a platter.

WISTMAN'S WOOD

RIVERS hasten to escape from Dartmoor; perhaps the Tavy deserves to escape, holding the English record for speed. No doubt Dartmoor was their prison, confining them in mire and quaking bog. Yet it was even more their parent; and some have done it credit, carving out a fine career and making a name for themselves, as the Lyd at Lydford Gorge. The Dart has given its name to Dartmouth, a famous naval port in Chaucer's time, though not in sight of the sea. It has even given its name to Dartmoor.

That is odd, parent named after offspring. But everything about Dartmoor is odd. On Shelldon Moor a double row of small stones, more than two miles long, appears to be the work of fairies, while the tors might be huge blocks of rock piled up by giants, such as Corin, who flung Gogmagog into the sea from Plymouth Hoe. No birds sing on the moor; apart from a lark singing high in heaven there is a deathlike silence; you feel you are on a dead planet. That there is something strange about Dartmoor, witness Wistman's Wood.

The Devon poet was proud of his oaks, 'a giant race', but here in the West Dart Valley

> a dwarfish race has risen,
> This pigmy grove.

Oaks show their strength by holding out heavy horizontal arms, but these oaks bend under wads of moss. Though of different ages, some still young, all are hoary with grey lichen, bowed and decrepit. Yet growing in a clitter of sharp angry rocks, they defy you to enter. Perhaps Wistman's is the only wood in England no one has ever crossed. If it is in England! Dartmoor has two other woods of the kind; where on earth could you find a fourth?

NEAR FOWEY

FROM THE HILLS behind Fowey you view a singular sight, mountains of the moon. Cone-shaped and silver, they are entrancing, but the streams that flow from them only a baby would admire. White as milk, they show what the lunar mountains are, the waste-heaps of Cornwall's china clay. Tristan's monument, a longstone standing at a crossroads, is as tell-tale as the milky streams.

How potent was the love philtre Tristan and Iseult drank; even Hodain, Tristan's hound, became more attached to his master by licking the cup. The jealous Mark thought it less punishment to banish his nephew than to put him to death, but Tristan died a thousand deaths each day. Perhaps Iseult was the truer lover; when he sent her Petitgru, the fairy dog with the golden bell whose tinkling eased the heart of all grief, she flung the bell into the sea. But both died of love; when Iseult, who had the greatest skill in medicine of her time, was summoned to heal Tristan's wounds, 'Tristan died of waiting, Iseult because she came too late'.

But the Tristan monument is tell-tale. Mark was not king of the two countries, Cornwall and England; he was a Celtic chieftain. He did not live at Tintagel in a castle chequered azure and cinnabar, the work of giants; he lived in an earthen camp with a long wooden building, Castle Dor. On the monument, which came from Castle Dor, he is not Tristan's uncle; he is his father! Perhaps the famous romance rose out of nothing more than the sad sound of the name, Tristan. But it would be none the worse for being moonshine like the lunar mountains, waste-heaps of exciting beauty.

THE ISLES OF SCILLY

THE ISLES OF SCILLY lie so low in the water that they appear to be sinking; your steamer might never arrive! You are relieved to find St. Mary's a substantial island. But burial cists found on shores and walls running aimlessly into the sea show that the Isles are sinking. They are also rising, for what the sea takes from the friable rock is added to bays and beaches. The land is encroaching on the sea.

Born of a mass of granite and the sea, the Isles form a family; but they have little family likeness; they might be different countries. All they have in common is a rich-coloured sea and its creatures. Common tern fly over it in twinkling flight, while shags stand on rocks in monkish meditation; a seal lifts its doglike head, dislikes your looks and disappears; you spy the sharp black fin of a basking shark, a lazy monster whose life is a long dinner of tiny fry.

The Isles owe much to the wind. Once it helped the sea to sink ships; nowhere does a bell-buoy toll over more drowned men; Round Island lighthouse is still ominous, flashing a bloodshot eye. Now it helps the land to raise flowers, wind-blown sand creating a light lively soil suited to early daffodils, anemones, ixias and arum lilies. Yet from the wind these have to be protected by tall hedges of veronica, tamarisk and pittosporum. Or by stone walls loosely built to allow them to be blown through rather than blown over; a sunset behind a wall fills its crevices with sparkling stones. A wind can only caress the small fields, breathing softly, 'A garden enclosed is my sister, my spouse.'

Yet the Isles seem less suited to the living than to the dead. They have many megalithic barrows, but few pre-historic artifacts have been found. The islands nearest the setting sun, the Bronze Age men saw in them the Fortunate Isles, where to be buried was yet in a way to be alive. 'Happy heroes, untouched by sorrow, they live along the shore of the deep-swirling ocean.' That seems possible in these paradoxical islands, sinking and rising.

CAERLEON-ON-USK

THE CITY OF LEGIONS has disappeared almost as completely as the legions themselves. Swans arching proud necks on the river are tame villatic fowl compared with the Roman triremes. But the name given to the amphitheatre, King Arthur's Round Table, speaks of a later Caerleon. It is still extant, for one can say,

Its creatures never were, and never will be not.

Of King Arthur we know next to everything; his sword was called Caledvwlch, his lance Rhongomyant, his shield Wynebswrthucher, and his three wives were all named Gwenhwyvar. We even know the name of his mantle, Gwern. One of the giants he overcame had a mantle made of the beards of kings he had slain; Gwern was made of diapered satin with apples of gold at the four corners. The land enjoyed great prosperity under his reign. Soldiers' arrows had shafts of ivory winged with peacock feathers. Chess-men were also of ivory and could play by themselves on their silver board. The Countess of the Fountain gave a feast which took three years to prepare and three months to consume. So blessed a reign could not end, even with Arthur's departure. Merlin embarked with Vivian in a ship and still sailed the sea, though the ship, made of glass, was invisible. Arthur was seen to embark, 'and it is believed he is yet alive, dwelling in Avalon with the fairest of all elves; and', adds Layamon, 'Britons look for Arthur's coming again'. Perhaps they forget about the elf.

SNOWDON

SNOWDON is very hospitable; a friendly octopus, it spreads the tentacles of its tracks to draw all men to its heart. The invitation you may regard as personal, for you can always be alone on Snowdon as you can in a crowded cathedral. Yet I cannot claim to have climbed Snowdon. Even though I were one of those cragsmen on Lliwedd who, body hanging by a rope and life by a thread,

> Look pleased, and make their danger their delight,

I should still feel that Snowdon was not for me.

It is no ordinary mountain. Majestic shape and setting make it look higher than it is; as much as the mind can take in, another thousand feet would not add a cubit to its stature. Yet to a Welshman it rises beyond itself, Eryri, Haunt of Eagles. 'Held sacred by the ancient *Britons*, as *Parnassus* by the *Greeks*, and *Ida* by the *Cretans*', it is still so held by their descendants. Others cannot share the feeling, and while they may be on the mountain, they are not on Snowdon. Many are the thyrsus-bearers, but few are the mystics.

One night I shall sleep on Snowdon. 'It is still said, that whoever sleeps on *Snowdon*, wakes inspired, as much as if he had taken a nap on the hill of *Apollo*.' Bidding the guide keep his eyes open for sunrise, Wordsworth took a nap and woke inspired to write,

> The moon hung naked in a firmament
> Of azure without cloud, and at my feet
> Rested a silent sea of hoary mist.

I can hardly hope to awake as a poet, but I might as—is there much difference?—a Welshman, at least by adoption, or as an initiate into the Cymric mysteries. Then at last I shall climb Snowdon; hitherto I have only reached the summit.

GRONGAR HILL

A MEDIEVAL ARCH in the garden of Aberglasney House, relic of a distant past, gave me the feeling that John Dyer and I were contemporaries; a man coming out of the house I should have taken for the poet. I might have asked him to point out Grongar Hill; for where was it,

> The windy summit, wild and high,
> Roughly rushing on the Sky?

At least, there was a rising road; it would give me a view of the Vale of Towy. It rose to the occasion.

The Vale has had a variety of celebrities, from Merlin, 'begotten by an Incubus Devill', to Jeremy Taylor who wrote *Holy Living* and *Holy Dying*. Dyer should have been a celebrity writing *The Fleece*; he could not have had a more inspiring subject than wool;

> hence Britannia sees
> Her solid grandeur rise.

But the verdict was 'he will be buried in woollen'. 'Odious! in woollen! 'twould a saint provoke.' But Dyer need not have been as alarmed as Mrs. Oldfield; he survives in *Grongar Hill*.

The roadside hedge was as in *The Fleece* 'white with woolly theft', and, sure enough, I came to a sheep-farm. Four ferocious dogs rushed at me, but all they wanted was to give me a kiss. The farmer's wife expected me; at least, she was accustomed to strangers asking the way to Grongar Hill. Soon I was on the hill, even enclosed in its Iron Age camp. The privilege! to stand where John had often stood, saying to himself,

> Ever charming, ever new,
> When will the Landskip tire the View!

Though *Grongar Hill* tells us nothing of the wonderful scene, it tells us everything: it could make a poet of John Dyer.

THE RED LADY OF PAVILAND

THE RED OCHRE, which stains her skeleton, is said to be an imitation of blood, imparting a specious immortality. Specious! I spent the best part of a week with the Lady. An ivory armlet had suggested a woman's skeleton; now it is said to be a young man's. And I slept with her each night in a cave! *A Guide to Gower* does not make the mistake: 'Leaping from crag to crag, the Red Lady of the Cavern goes bounding on with wild and discordant screams, her long red mantle streaming weirdlike in the ghastly light of the sickly moon.' But how unlike the Lady I met on Yellow Top!

Under the headland was Paviland Cave, where also were discovered the remains of an elephant. We never descended; her burial-place had memories for her, having been her home. Our walks were mainly on the cliffs. One morning, however, I took her to Arthur's Stone on Cefn-y-Bryn, imagining a monument three or four thousand years old might edge me a little closer to her Paleolithic Age; but she was not interested; to anyone buried in a cave a Bronze Age cromlech may seem ultra-modern. Another time we walked on Rossili Down, but she was unaffected by its charm; the climate tropical in her day, stunted heather was a poor substitute for the jungle into which she had ventured as a girl, and rabbits were small deer compared with the animals her father trapped. She told me that after living for days on nuts, shell-fish and snails they made a great feast of a trapped animal. That night such a feast we had ourselves in our cave; if I remember rightly, the rhinoceros was tough, but of the elephant little was left.

Our parting was sudden. We had come round Brandy Cove to a cliff overlooking Pwll-du Bay. It was full of blue pebbles. Perhaps the Red Lady had an antipathy to blue, for she vanished. I felt it was more than a personal loss; I was bereaved of the adorable name, the Red Lady of Paviland. 'What's in a name?' asked Juliet; she could not have cared greatly for her Romeo.

RADNORSHIRE HILLS

RADNORSHIRE has fine Tudor and Jacobean houses; they seem suited to a county where English, not Welsh, is spoken. It has charming magpie buildings, black and white, but cheerful in their half-mourning. It has won fame by its rood-screens, Old Radnor's screen so rich in grape clusters that it keeps harvest festival throughout the year. But the county's chief architectural interest is in its hills.

Radnorshire hills behave in an odd way. In one group they strike attitudes, posing as mountains; perhaps it is because they are near the English border, though anything might be expected of hills with such names as Smatcher, Squilver and Cowlod. But they are pastoral, breeding enough lambs to warm the heart of Blake and with no dark Satanic mills to call for his burning bow; for these the wool goes to Bradford. All they share with mountains are wide views, which make it worth while coming to Wales to see England. You might feel you have left the better land behind, but the fat Herefordshire plain cannot compare with Radnorshire's rocky dingles; 'the sweetest flesh is nearest the bone.'

But if these hills by putting on acts flatter themselves they are mountains, hills of another group, Radnor Forest, make a mock pretence of being moors. Their tops are as broad as their bottoms; on Great Rhos you can walk for miles through heather and sun-burnished bracken, the hillsides out of sight. Only the Whimble rises to a cone, so inclined that you can pick bilberries, called whimberries, almost without stooping. The scene is so primordial, that you are surprised to find youself there. Yet you are not lonely, having an unusual preoccupation with your own company. If even that grows tedious in time, you can lose yourself in an oakwood dingle. There you will find company in the dingle rill; though cold, it will give

you a warm, even gushing welcome. But not always; sometimes it is tired and listless. That is in summer,

> When dingle rills grow dumber,
> Till only sand and gravel
> Show sullen pools the way to travel,
> And little water flows
> But what by root and tree-trunk goes,
> Sinking and rising up
> To vein a leaf or fill an acorn's cup.

ST. DAVID'S

WHAT St. David cultivated in Vallis Rosina was not roses, but himself, and 'with what a blaze of miracles he shone'. Water even more helpful in the cultivation of saints than of roses, 'he, rejecting wine and beer, lived as a fish lives in water'; he was David of the Aquatic Life, and his companions were the Watermen. Of course, they had to cultivate the land as well, but that was made to serve their own cultivation; 'they placed the yoke on each other's shoulders; each man, to himself and his brethren, was an ox.' They were not anchorites like the Welsh saints, for whom an island in the sea was the same as the Egyptian desert, a howling wilderness; paths led from their narrow valley to the surrounding land, a wide plateau that, austere and full of sky, is suitably named after St. David, Dewisland. He himself travelled far afield; he became so popular a saint that all Welshmen are named after him, Taffy, the Welsh pronunciation of Davy.

Yet St. David's seems remote from men; no other cathedral in Christendom is so far from the centre of the diocese. And it hides itself in Vallis Rosina; viewed from the village, smallest of cities, it appears with a palace as large as Lambeth to be lying in a ditch; with a long leap you could land on the tower. To enter needs a kind of priestly induction; you descend steps known as the Thirty-nine Articles. And everything about the cathedral is queer. It is purple, as though still mourning over the saint's tomb. The nave has a sloping floor, the surprise, if not the slope, making you giddy. The roof might fall on you any moment, for the pier-arcades lean outwards, as though thrust apart by an invisible Samson. St. David's shrine has strange openings, where sick people slept through the night to be near his bones. They hoped to be healed, and perhaps they were; in so queer a cathedral even a saint's bones cannot be completely at rest.

THE LADY ON THE LAWN

SUDDENLY I KNEW who the lonely figure was, the
Matchless Orinda. She gazed sadly at the Priory; it had
been more than a home, a Temple. The learned Palaemon,

> who might be
> Esteem'd himself an University,

had discovered Friendship;

> he's our original,
> That made Friends more than Lovers burn.

The Priory had become the Temple of Friendship, herself
the Priestess. She had prophesied,

> pilgrims shall ten ages hence
> Approach our Tombs with reverence.

Alas, I was the only pilgrim.

She turned to view me with enquiring eyes: 'Was you a
Friend?' Somehow the old-fashioned grammar put an idea
in my head: if I was the ghost she took me to be, I might
have been a Friend. It seemed only half a lie to nod my
head. Then remembering that Friends had adopted names
—Palaemon's real name was Finch—I told the whole lie:
'I was Juvenal.' 'You have returned to visit some scene,

> A Rock which civil Nature made a seat,
> A Brook which sobbed aloud and ran away,

some dear scene where you and another, tasting Love's
Elixir, became compasses?' Knowing that by compasses she
meant Friends,

> That are, and yet they are not, two,

I half-nodded. Then after a pause 'I came to climb a mountain', I said, adding to make it sound more likely for a
ghost, 'by night'. As she looked at me with great surprise,

I explained, 'I mean Cader Idris; if you climb it by night, one of three things will happen.' Her wonder changed to interest. 'You will be dead by dawn.' 'But I am dead', she said. 'Or you will go mad.' 'But I should be mad to climb a mountain by day.' 'Or you will become a poet.' Giving a start, she exclaimed, '*Become* a poet!' I saw my mistake and cried, 'Of course, my dear, you are a poet, hailed as our English Sappho.' But I cried it to the empty air.

YOUNG WILL

HAMLET'S MOTHER KNEW that a wood-pigeon's chicks
are 'golden couplets', but young Will, not the lady, climbed
the trees. Perhaps he did worse than steal birds' eggs; he
could not have said like young Macduff, 'small birds they
are not set for'; the Plays are so full of gins, bird-lime, nets,
springes, pitfalls, bird-bolts, stone-bows and birding-pieces
that they make painful reading. And the Forest of Arden
had other attractions than birds.

> Creeping like snail
> Unwillingly to school,

he could hear

> the musical confusion
> Of hounds and echo in conjunction,

and could not resist 'such gallant chiding', 'such sweet
thunder'. Worse than the gins, bird-lime and the like are
the hunting hounds, flew'd, dew-lapp'd, sanded, crook-
knee'd, causing the pained reader to cry out at last,

> get thee away, and take
> Thy beagles with thee.

The holidays had other interests for Will than watching

> poor Wat
> Stand on his hinder legs with listening ear.

One summer the Queen stayed at Kenilworth, and when
his father announced that as chief alderman of Stratford he
would attend the celebrations, there was no holding back
the boy of eleven. There was a water-pageant: 'Proteus
appeared, sitting on a *Dolphyns* backe; within the which
Dolphyn a Consort of Musicke was secretly placed.' What
Will recalled in later life was

> a mermaid on a dolphin's back,

and not a consort but a song, dulcet and harmonious breath. And there were fireworks, 'then thought extremely wonderful';

> And certain stars shot madly from their spheres.

At Whitsun it was always a joy for Will to visit Aunt Joan. She lived on the Cotswolds, and if he found

> Those high wild hills and rough uneven ways
> Draw out the miles,

they were shortened by the thought of what was in store; in his aunt's town, Barton-on-the-Heath, were held at Whitsun the Dover Games, 'England's Olympicks'. How he spent his Easter holidays the Plays do not tell. Perhaps the schoolboy was already finding

> Such comfort as do lusty young men feel,
> When well-apparell'd April on the heel
> Of limping winter treads.

Young Will may have been old for his years.

THE STAIRCASE

GOING up the staircase, I said, 'Yes, she was innocent', and coming down, 'No'. This went on throughout the day. Mary came down the staircase one winter morning to find a great fire burning in the banqueting-hall and Bull, the masked headsman, standing by a black-draped scaffold. That was the real staircase, still extant as staircase of The Talbot; what I went up and down was a ghostly image. Coming down I thought,

> Queens should be cold and wise,
> And she loved little things,
> Parrots,
> And red-legged partridges.

When Bull removed her garters, he found a little dog under her dress. Coming down, I thought of her playing golf and pall-mall with Bothwell a few days after Darnley's murder. Going up, I remembered that Bull burnt all her clothing lest it should provide the relics of a martyr and a saint. Coming down, I felt that she was implicated to the neck, the stiff neck that it took three blows of Bull's axe to sever. So it went on till evening, when I went out to Fotheringhay. The castle was gone, the floor of the banqueting-hall having disclosed its secret to heaven; only the great mound remained. I felt the trees on its steep slope leaned towards it sympathetically.

> Why, since Dodona's holy Oak,
> Have trees been dumb and never spoke?

They might have told me something that there and then would have sent me bounding up the staircase. Later it would have made me glad to feel, going to my bedroom in The Talbot, that I was sharing Mary's staircase, even wish that I might also share her bed.

AT GRIME'S GRAVES

BRECKLAND is England's desert; tall hedges protect it
from sand-storms; something warns you to beware of
vipers, the abundant viper's bugloss, reputed to drive them
away, not reassuring; plants from the Russian steppes have
settled in the Breck. Yet here was Britain's main indus-
trial region; you can descend mines, where men worked
with red deer antlers for picks and oxens' shoulder-blades
for shovels. The ground is still strewn with flint-knappers'
chips.

It seemed an unlikely place to seek inspiration for a
poem, even on a moonlit night. And at first none came;
I could only tax my brain with the laboured result:

> The flints that on the warren lie,
> Glinting with snaky eye,
> Though chipped by knappers for flint arrows
> That flew away like sparrows,
> Are still so fresh that one might say
> The dead men were on holiday.
> Few poems keep as fresh as flints,
> The green-eyed moonlight hints—

Here suddenly the inspiration came; perhaps my stumbling
about among the warren's dark humps and hollows relaxed
my mind to receive it, something I could not have said
myself—

> Yours will not last as long;
> They will not even go for an old song.

FENLAND

FENLAND has no fens, or only the preserved Wicken Fen.
Though it is flat—

> The sky is all around
> And creeps in dykes along the ground—

clouds soaring from the horizon give it a mountainous appearance. Islands like the Isle of Ely are entirely surrounded by land, and rivers like the Bedfords are as high as your head. These with the lesser drains, cuts, eaus, leams and lodes are water-carriers, discouraged by the level ground. The Cam's case is sad; entertaining Cambridge undergraduates in a way hardly becoming Milton's 'Camus, reverend sire', it is reduced in Fenland to a poor canal; willows in the Backs weep over its departure.

Draining has sunk Fenland to a lower level, while raising it to a higher value. But low land is a temptation to water, and people remember the flood that appeared one morning at their bedroom windows. Some day Fenland will revert to its former state, a waste of water-ways and islands, the air flapped by swallow-tailed butterflies, cranes and ospreys sailing overhead, bitterns booming from the rushes. People will dart about in all directions, catching the wind in their sails or making their own rushing wind on skates. Their life will be one long sporting event, shooting wild-fowl and fishing. Some birds they will spare, spoonbills, avocets and black-tailed godwits, and some fish they will not eat, devil-fish and blood-sucking lampreys. Of eels, that gave their name to Ely, they may tire in time, but perhaps not. Formerly rentals and tithes could be paid in eels, and some old law might be evoked to allow income-tax to be paid in eels. Their amphibious life will have its hazards, but in March's church-roof hover over a hundred angels waiting to waft them to heaven; their wooden wings are already outspread.

ON THE BROADS

No YACHTSMAN, whose delight is to recline in a half-capsized boat within an inch of being drowned, I hired a rowing-boat. For three days I rowed about, making no progress, so erratic are the rivers, blinded by bushes, in their search for the sea. It was early in the season, more warblers in the reed-beds than on the wireless. A few motor-boats passed, panting with unnecessary haste and agitating the water-lily pads. There were also yachts, which did not pant, though labouring along like big-bellied women. It was odd to see a landscape with sails moving in different directions. Though all was new and strange, I had the feeling of something very old, yet familiar. These sluggish rivers and meres belonged to an earlier world; they spoke to a primal part of my being, a little frightening to my later, sophisticated self.

Different was my experience on Rockland Broad, remote and lonely. Watched by a ghostly heron perched on a pole, I followed Wordsworth's example at Ullswater and stole a boat.

> Water too clear to show
> Without a frown, ruffling its brow

I knew was water, churning it with my oars; otherwise it did not exist. Crested grebes dived down into nowhere. I was in mid air; as a drop fell from my suspended oar, a drop rose from an oar below the boat;

> They met to perish in a kiss.

I hung between earth and heaven; if at Heigham Broad and Horsey Mere I was subhuman, on Rockland Broad I was an elevated saint.

LIZARD ORCHID

ORCHIDS LOOK ODD, the flowers being upside down. Bog orchid is an exception, but hardly to be congratulated on having its head screwed on the right way; the flower has been given a second twist, so that it is only right by being doubly wrong. Some orchids have another oddity, the likeness to an animal. The monkey orchid is a poor ape, but in the fly orchid 'only the buzz is missing'. In the man orchid we see a little man being hanged, arms and legs dangling pathetically in the air. In the lizard orchid we see a bunch of lizards. It is so rare that a dried specimen was left me in a will.

The soldier orchid, its uniform red and white, was long thought to be a deserter. When it was rediscovered by a friend, I looked for such an invitation as Fronto gave Marcus Aurelius: 'Maybe, my boy, you would like to see the flower; well, let us go for a walk as far as the Illysus'; but either he was no Fronto or he did not regard me as a Marcus Aurelius. That he refused to show me the very rare plant raised him in my estimation; since then, however, he has sunk.

How different was Miss Talbot! Contriving to let the other members of the botanical party go well ahead of us, she said 'Come' and darted into a scrubby wood. It was a lizard orchid! How anxious she was to show it to a stranger, while careful not to arouse the others' curiosity about the wood. But it was about herself they were curious. When we rejoined them later, picnicking under trees, they recieved us with a studied silence. That Miss Talbot of all people should have walked off with the handsome stranger!

LATHKILL DALE

Approaching Lathkill Dale from Monyash, you see nothing to suggest a dale; the low hills could not provide one and no river is in sight. But you begin to descend with the hills growing higher on either side,

> Hills scattered with grey limestone rocks,
> Their old unchanging flocks;

you are even privileged to witness the river's birth, a cave the open womb. Boulders begin to block your way, warning you of some infernal region; but continuing to descend you find youself, a second Aeneas, in a valley of the underworld, winding through it a fairer Styx. You descend so deep into the earth that, holding back your head, you see a village high above the trees. It has a celestial look; Over Haddon could not have an inn that sold beer. The river is now so far beneath the earth's surface that it can have no hope of ever reaching the sea; it might as well turn back. It halts, forming fish-pools, rich with water vegetation, pools to which Solomon might better have compared the Shulamite's eyes than to the fish-pools of Heshbon. And sometimes the river does turn back; taking a vacation from its summer course, it retreats to the cool shelter of its native cave. Then the river-bed becomes a flower-bed, blue geraniums richly compensating for the want of water. Flowers or water, either shows that Lathkill Dale is no infernal region; with other Derbyshire dales it is England's effort to draw her lovers to her heart.

THE GREEN KNIGHT'S
CHAPEL

WHEN CHARLES COTTON gazed down into the deep Eldon Hole, he was so aghast that his hair lifted his hat; at Ludchurch or, as it is called, The Green Knight's Chapel, his hat would have flown off his head. In the narrow rock fissure, its vertical walls more than fifty feet high, the intruder feels himself half-swallowed by the earth. It was a suitable scene for Sir Gawain's second encounter with the Green Knight. The first was at the New Year festival at Camelot; there he slashed off the Green Knight's head. When the Green Knight picked the head from the floor and held it by the hair, the eyes looked glaringly at Queen Guinevere. Perhaps it was for her sake that, the head having been replaced, he made a vow to meet the Green Knight at the Chapel in a year and a day to receive blow for blow. Sir Gawain found the Chapel a most evil holy place, a hideous oratory, where Satan might be seen saying mattins at midnight. And he knew that once his head was off, it was off for ever. But the Green Knight allowed the axe merely to graze his neck. As the slight wound was a penance, Ludchurch, so far from being an evil place, is a true chapel. Yet the intruder may not feel reassured till, making a hurried escape, he sees the green fields of the Dane Valley smiling to him through the trees, and hears the river laughing.

NORTHUMBERLAND

A SENTRY on the Roman Wall felt he was at a terminus, the world's end. You might have the same feeling, verdant country behind you and in front the Wastes. These stretch to where moor and mountain, mingling outlines, give the land an indeterminate look. Other things are indeterminate: Holy Island is, as the Venerable Bede said, 'an island only twice a day'; climbing the Cheviot you find its summit an enormous bog and look up to the sky for another summit; the wild white cattle you view from a distance in Chillingham Park might be the ghosts of ancient aurochs.

Yet the buildings have an intense look. Castles frown at you; pele-towers and bastel-houses give you a hard stare; fortified farmhouses and church-towers are watchful; 'An Englishman's house is his castle', says the Embleton parson. The stone rings dangling on hill-tops are not ornaments, but Iron Age camps. Bewcastle has a Roman fort, a castle, a church and a famous cross, but there is no village; in its churchyard only women are buried, their husbands hanged elsewhere. Men-at-arms on the barbican of Alnwick Castle, and even the lion on the Lion Bridge, still look to the North, petrified by an ancient fear.

Out of the north wind grief came forth—

Caledonians, Picts and Scots—

And the shining of a sword out of the sea—

Danes and Saxons. These invaders have created a strange peace. It is positive, felt more in the banqueting-hall of Warkworth Castle than in the rock-hewn Hermitage up the river. Northumberland, its very name a battle-shout, is the most peaceful county in England.

SOLWAY FIRTH

WOODS that come down to the sea, lit by rhododendrons and red and pink hawthorn blossom, beaches silver with bleached cockle-shells, heathy headlands and isle-studded inlets, Gatehouse-of-Fleet with its painted houses and Kirkcudbright, 'the Venice of Scotland', all backed by a dominating mountain, Cairnsmore of Fleet, nothing is wanting to the Solway Firth, unless it is the sea. Then there is empty desert. Gay colours do not save the yachts at Kippford from having a dejected look as they recline on the mud-banks, hopeless of the tide's return. But the emptiness itself is singular, neither land nor sea. And wet sands can be shot with glancing lights and mud is receptive of heavenly hues. And of earthly at sunset;

> Muddy creeks the tide has worn
> Shine as with purple grapes and golden corn.

A distant sound announces that the Solway is about to stage its famous spectacle, the tide's return. Presently it appears, a long low wall of surf, moaning to itself, as it is pushed from behind by a multitude of impatient waves. When it comes closer, it appears so swift and yet so stealthy, so deliberate in its infiltration, that you have the queer feeling of something other than water, a live creature, snaky and sinister. It is wise to keep out of its way, for the Solway does not like trespassers.

GREY GALLOWAY

THOUGH YOU VIEW with surprise Loch Trool, a High-land-looking loch in the Lowlands, to reach the heart of Grey Galloway, if it has a heart, you have to climb to Loch Enoch, interviewing two other lochs on the way. There you feel alone as never before. Yet you are not alone; if you see a grey boulder moving along a mountain slope, you know it is a sheep. Rocks look freshly streaked by glaciers, as though the Ice Age ended in the spring. All is as remote in time as in space. Loch Enoch lies among mountains, but so high on their slopes that it reduces them to hills. Shaped like an octopus, it contains an island, which contains a loch, Loch-in-Loch. There is no lack of lochs; you cannot climb a mountain without being watched by their glassy eyes.

If Loch Enoch is the heart of Grey Galloway, what you view far below is the entrails, the Dungeon. Though it is an open prison, you would take hours to break out in a mist. There are no roads, only the Lanes, travelled by fish, burns linking loch with lonely loch. In floods they flash a silver light, but usually the most cheerful things you see are the death-pale lochs. But the strange scene is more widely viewed from a mountain range on the other side. There you would not feel lonely, though you were by yourself. Carlin's Cairn, Conserine, Millfire and Meikle Millyea, these mountains are great friends, linked arm in arm; and they would be friendly with you, raising no difficulty to your walking over their heads and shoulders, miles of easy perambulation.

MELROSE ABBEY

WHEN Lady Alice sat at her bower-window,

>   she saw as fine a corpse,
> As ever she saw in her life;

so one might view the beautiful ruin, Melrose Abbey.
But corpse or not, it must look askance at the Tweed, that
fair but faithless river that born and bred in Scotland goes
over to England. For it remembers the Border warfare
that aroused an interest in Paradise. The Eagle spoke of it
to Dante, and even he may have been shocked. There was
the fair Lilliard's case at Ancrum Moor:

> And when her legs were cuttit off,
> She fought upon her stumps.

In the Scottish Border country are no old towns. Only
Roxburgh was saved from the English; the Scots destroyed
it themselves, a Royal Burgh. The benty hills and copses
of drooping birch have a pensive look.

But Melrose Abbey has a reddish hue, as though warmed
by more refreshing memories. Even at Flodden

> The stubborn spearmen still made good
> Their dark impenetrable wood;

at Otterburn the Douglas had his dream, a true pre-
monition,

> I saw a dead man win a fight
> And I think that man was I.

Shakespeare speaks of 'the weasel Scot' but the 'weasel' did
not cross the border to catch a mouse according to the
Northumbrian lament:

> We'll sune hae neither cow nor ewe,
> We'll sune hae neither staig nor stot.

When her cupboard was becoming bare, the Flower of Yarrow laid a pair of spurs on her husband's breakfast table; then when the moon shone,

> Ye might see by its light in Harden glen
> A bow o' kye and a bassen'd bull.

Auld Wat even shook his head at a haystack: 'By my soul, had ye but four feet ye should not stand lang there.' In Melrose Abbey lies the Wondrous Wizard, Michael Scot; Dante saw him in Purgatory, his head turned round for peering into the future. It turns the head of a Border Scot to look back on the past.

DWARF BIRCH

MORE THAN HALF in love with silver birch I had a desire to meet the little sister, dwarf birch. Little sister! in this country it is a tree of great antiquity, going back to the Ice Age. Friends introduced me to it in their Sussex garden, a plant brought from a grouse moor in Sutherland. Its diminutive size, three feet tall, was charming; I longed for its more intimate acquaintance on some native heath.

In my Highland wanderings I stared at hundreds of birches about three feet tall, but they were children, not dwarfs. At last I learned that on a low slope of Beinn a' Bhuird, between the Slugan Burn and the Quoich Water, grew a forest of dwarf birches. Making my way to the forest I met a small plant, *chamaepericlymenum suecicum*, dwarf cornel for short. I compared it unfavourably with the dwarf I was about to see. Like its Japanese relation, aucuba, it paints and powders itself; I preferred the simpler charm of little catkins and lacquered leaves. Perhaps it tries to keep up appearances, for once a shrub like common cornel it has come down in the world; dwarf birch, though only three feet tall, maintains its status as a tree.

But where was the forest I had come to see? Between the Slugan Burn and the Quoich Water was bare moorland, cut up by peat-hags. Gazing all around I said,

> Nothing is here but black peat-hags,
> Where a slow Lethe drags.

But as I advanced among them, watching my step, I suddenly saw I was in the forest. I was surrounded by dwarf birches, tiny trees about three inches high. The plant in the southern garden had grown to an unnatural height; three feet seemed too tall for a tree.

THE BAD STEP

If like Sancho Panza you would own an island, nothing prevents your having one of the Western Isles; Wordsworth is said to have owned the Lake District as though the title-deeds were in his pocket. Your only difficulty might be in the choice. Seil might scarcely seem an island, connected with the mainland by a bridge, claimed to be the only bridge across the Atlantic, while the Garvelloch Isles might seem too insular, their other name, Isles of the Sea, hardly tautological. If you were addicted to both whisky and milk, you would choose Islay, though viewing across the Sound the famous Paps,

> Breasts that rise soft and round,
> Not two but three,

you might become enamoured of Jura. There, however, hooting deer off its road, you might feel that to them the title-deeds properly belonged.

Perhaps your best choice would be Arran. Though it lies south of the English town, Berwick-on-Tweed, it is a pocket version of the Western Highlands, and with the title-deeds in your pocket you would be proud. Its majestic mountains are very approachable, two glens offering an immedate introduction. Glen Sannox looks stern, but Glen Rosa is friendly, fuchsias, roses and rhododendrons giving you a warm welcome. Yet you have not gone far before it becomes forbidding, as though you were going too far. Perhaps of something on the ridge opposite Goatfell it is saying, 'Watch your step'. The view from the ridge is almost frightening; their calm air of majesty thrown off, the mountains appear naked and savage. But the ridge offers you a safe and easy track. It gradually narrows, however, till it is broken by a gap, Mauvais Pas, the Bad Step. One stride will take you across the gap, but if you lose your head, you will also lose your life, falling hundreds of feet below. That would be a pity, if you had already lost your heart to Arran and, the title-deeds in your pocket, you were as rich as that poor man, Wordsworth.

IONA

It is odd that a half-blind scribe should have written Iona instead of Ioua, for iona is in Hebrew what columba is in Latin, dove. Dove suits the little island that endears itself with its white sands and tiny mountain with a cone, Dun I; but it seems less suited to St. Columba, who in Ireland had the nickname Crimthain or Wolf. Perhaps he owed it to his voice, which could be heard a mile away; when he frightened the Loch Ness monster, as St. Adamnan relates, he may only have shouted. Yet seals raised their heads from the water, when he sang to them in Iona, sitting on the rocks. He was no wolf to the Irish children who ran to greet him, but Columcille, Dove of the Cell or Church Pigeon.

But St. Columba was more, a carrier pigeon. Another Dove, Jonah or Iona, rather than preach to the people of Nineveh, paid his passage to Spain; St. Columba set sail to preach to the Scots of Alba. Both composed a poem on the voyage, Jonah in the whale's belly, St. Columba in his coracle.

> Large is the tear in my soft grey eye,
> When I look back on Erin,

he sang. And Iona he found more suited to a rock pigeon than to a wood pigeon.

> Crowded full of heaven's angels
> Is every leaf of the oaks of Derry,
> My Derry, my little oak-grove,
> My dwelling and my little cell;

but there were no angels in Iona's scrubby trees. His twelve companions saw angels, but they were hovering around his head, as he pointed his hands in prayer. But he was no homing pigeon to return to Erin; he fell in love with the island:

89

Ioua of my heart,
Ioua of my love.

And his mission prospered; his name became known 'not only throughout Britain, the world's largest island, but reaching Rome, the chief of all cities'. A dove lays two eggs, but this Dove hatched a miraculous brood; 'from the nest of Columba those sacred doves took their flight to all quarters'. The saint himself took his flight in the end; his body is not in Iona and, as is said of Moses, 'no man knoweth of his sepulchre unto this day'. Perhaps that was appropriate for a saint who in this world was only a bird of passage.

ON A SUTHERLAND MOUNTAIN

'But you cannot climb a mountain in these', I said, meaning her shoes made of fine leather and stockings of nothing; 'Why not', Sweetie asked. Though I felt I could safely leave the matter to the mountain, I wished I had called the plant mugwort, not Artemisia Norvegica, or had told them of my vow to reveal to no one its whereabouts. I even wished I had not accepted Tom's offer to drive me to the mountain foot.

On the stalkers' path Sweetie led the way. 'If a Footman puts *Mugwort* in his shoes in the Morning, he may goe forty Miles before Noon and not be weary.' She had put mugwort in her fine shoes; Artemis, famous huntress over mountains, could hardly have gone faster. But struggling through tough heather, 'Oh, dear!' she cried and sought comfort in a cigarette. 'You cannot smoke climbing a mountain, I protested.' 'Why not?' she replied; 'I smoke when I am having babies.' Artemis used mugwort to assist women at child-birth; it is out of date in midwifery. Tom was the one who would have turned back, but his wife was his mistress.

As we approached the summit, which I had never imagined they would approach, I became concerned about my vow. When we reached the cairn, Sweetie still had mugwort in her shoes, but Tom flung himself down with 'I am dying'. 'Good', I said to him, and to her, 'Look after him well', and darted off in the wrong direction. But hoping to mislead Sweetie, I misled myself. Where was the boulder I was told to look out for? I sadly reflected that I could not fail to keep my vow. Suddenly I saw it, a poor object, strangely unconscious of being named after a goddess and one of the world's rarest plants. As I knelt beside it, I heard a joyful cry, 'I am coming'. Having no time to think, I had an inspiration. At hand grew mountain solidago; I could pass it off as the plant and keep my vow.

But as she stood beside me, I saw from the corner of my eye her shoes and stockings; they were my undoing; I could not resist the temptation to tell Sweetie the truth.

UNCERTAIN MOUNTAINS

ON THE CAIRNGORMS you appear to be on a plateau; the impression is less of rising mountains than of sinking glens. Other Highland mountains have a stronger personality. Ben Cruachan shouts its name, the Campbells' war-cry, down Loch Awe. The Five Sisters of Kintail are so unlike one another that they might not be distant relations. Liathach, the Grey One, has an anguished look, its rocks in tortured shapes and its precipices falling away in sheer despair. Ben More Assynt, made of the rock, Old Boy, claims to be the world's oldest mountain, the Alps mere upstarts. The Black Cuillin have even an infernal character; climbers on a rock-face have been heard to say,

> It would not kill me though I fell;
> On you, Black Cuillin, I am now in hell.

Yet all these mountains are of uncertain character; they often lose their heads in a mist; they may even vanish into thick air. With the Black Cuillin in Skye, Ossian's Isle of Mist, the habit is so common that you imagine they have their visiting days.

But mountains near the coast have a stranger uncertainty; they are uncertain what they are. So far from sulking in a mist they become visionary. It happens on evenings when the sea itself suffers a sea-change, water changed to wine, so that Homer would not speak of the unvintaged sea. Then, too, every sea-loch has its own sunset. In an atmosphere tinged with purple the mountains are no longer rock and earth; they are unsubstantial, their own rich pictures. Anyone witnessing this transfiguration has already 'an handsome anticipation of heaven'.

ORKNEY AND SHETLAND

THE ISLANDER speaks of sailing or flying to Scotland. Lerwick has a queer foreign look; its streets are all pavement, shared by buses, perambulators and people. King Hakon Street and King Harald Street are not named after Scottish kings. If Orkney and Shetland are a part of Scotland, England, not separated by the sea, is even more a part.

Shetland has the stronger character; though invaded by voes, it rebuffs the sea with cliffs three times the size of the Cornish cliffs. It is mainly a black character, much of mainland covered with peat-hags and one island so savagely cut for peats that it answers to its wild name, Yell. There are islands called Papa, as Papa Stour, Great Priest's Island, but the land has a heathenish look. It seems no time since Pictish chieftains built the brochs, forts that look like dovecots.

For a boreal archipelago Orkney looks surprisingly green. Yet cows abound, and nothing gives more colour to a landscape than a cow. North Ronaldsay has a wall to keep the sheep off the grass, too rich for the northern breed except at lambing time. There are a few trees; they are unlikely to be true Orcadians, for at prehistoric Skara Brae not only the huts, but their beds, tables and other furniture as well, are all of stone. But Orkney's greatest surprise is small cyclones that find a path on its glacier-flattened surfaces. A valley can have two kinds of weather, one side dark with mist, the other white with wisps of sunny cloud. The valley might be showing a conjuring trick, except that it looks as bewildered as yourself. That, of course, might be part of the trick; Orkney may not be as green as it looks.

THE HESPERIDES

POETS HAVE MADE Hebrides a magic word; sailing for
the Outer Isles you hope to light on the Hesperides. The
Barra Islands look strange, but they are hills half-sunk in
the sea. And once gigantic waves heaving against the six-
hundred-foot cliff of Barra Head left small fish on its
summit; there are no such storms in the Isles of the Blest.
South Uist is mainly rocks, bogs and lochans. The lochans
are lively in the wind, tossing white water-lilies and mute
swans, but the island has a half-created look, land and
water not fully separated and vegetation scarcely begun.
Benbecula, its low flat neighbour, appears to be rising from
the sea; and it is subject to mirages, a beach tilted like a
cliff and off-shore an islet hanging in the air; it is a small
piece of creation still unstable. North Uist is even nearer
chaos; it has a road, and there are peat-tracks, but you
would need wings to explore the watery wilderness. Harris
and Lewis are not islands, unless they are Siamese twins.
Mountains and long sea-lochs give Harris a grandeur un-
suited to human beings, at least more suited to red deer and
seals, while in Lewis the Callernish Stones, that in their
lonely setting make Stonehenge seem suburban, have a
heathenish look; neither could be an Isle of the Blest.

But you need not lose hope of the Hesperides, least of all
in North Uist with its Machair Leathann. A machair is
merely flat land and a sandy shore, but the one is so verdant
and the other so snowy, that spring and winter rub
shoulders. The sea only shows itself when it breaks into
white ripples; on the beach you step into invisible pools.
But some evenings the sea becomes jovial, opal near the
shore, turquoise farther out, and where it meets the sky,
mocking it with cobalt blue. But that adds nothing to the
machair; it takes from it, spoiling the appearance of something fresh from creation, simple and very beautiful. A
machair by itself would be a Hesperis.